A FIELD GUIDE TO GEEZERS

An Illustrated Look
at a Curious Branch of Hominids

A book of humor

by Rae Ellen Lee
with illustrations by John A. Alley

Rae Ellen Lee

This guide is dedicated with great affection to my father, Wesley Moore, alias Post Hole Augerson, (1906–1990) and to all other "greatest generation" geezers. Members of this rare species are often bespectacled, loquacious, and humble, and you can still meet them at all-you-can-eat pancake breakfasts. One I met had come ashore at Omaha Beach. Another knew the locations of the only remaining B-36 bombers in the world, and he had visited all four of them.

DISCLAIMER

Let's get one thing straight. This guide is based on fraudulent and shoddy research methods. Serious geezer *aficionados* might go so far as to call the work a hoax. Think of it as a grass-roots attempt to share anecdotal evidence, turned up during decades of observation. The author is also not engaged in rendering legal or other professional services, and shall have neither liability nor responsibility for time wasted by use of material contained in this book.

GREAT BLUE GRAPHICS
Book cover design by Kate Weisel,
www.weiselcreative.com

CONTENTS

Also by Rae Ellen Lee

I Only Cuss When I'm Sailing — A memoir
(First published as *If* The Shoe *Fits*)

My Next Husband Will Be Normal
– A St. John Adventure
Memoir/Sequel to *I Only Cuss When I'm Sailing*

The Bluebird House –
A Brothel. A Diary. A Murder.
A novel set in Montana

Cheating the Hog –
A Sawmill. A Tragedy. A Few Gutsy Women.
A novel dedicated to women working in the
trades.

Powder Monkey Tales — *A Portrait in Stories*
(As told by Wesley Moore
alias Post Hole Augerson)

PART 1

INTRODUCTION

Geezers evolved toward the end of the Mesozoic Era in what is now central Europe. While dinosaurs were going extinct left and right, mammals made dramatic evolutionary developments. Some of the special hominids that climbed down out of the trees back then looked a lot like some of us living in North America today. Geezer watching is booming in popularity. With census statistics showing that forty-one per cent of U. S. citizens are over the age of forty-five, you'll often find a geezer right under your nose.

Like birds, geezers generate interest because of all the colorful species. Recognition is step number one in any branch of natural science, and the knowledge you gain in this guide will make initial recognition easier. Many individuals have idiosyncratic features or patterns of behavior that can only be considered bizarre. Some are shy and withdrawn, while others are highly social and proud to be outrageous. He (or she) might be oblivious to their status, but a geezer in denial is a geezer nonetheless.

One important caveat: not every person of advanced age who appears to have jumped the fence of normalcy qualifies as a geezer.

As an amateur naturalist and geezer enthusiast, my research is based on years of firsthand encounters and an extensive collection of field notes on sightings, sounds, footprints, behaviors, ranges, and territories. I listened to their tales and fables, tracked their daily routines and, ignoring the warnings of friends, I willingly followed a few of them home. Doing so gave me the opportunity to watch them wake up in the morning. Then, too, I've worked with more than a few specimens, and while no federal funds were used in conducting research for this guide, I will admit to being paid for time spent observing them. No one warned me, however, to beware of geezer molecules, so I am permanently altered by these experiences. Or call it synchronicity, but I learned the hard way that it is alarmingly easy to acquire geezer tendencies.

After studying this guide and the illustrations, you'll be able to recognize a geezer up to a mile away. A good pair of binoculars or a spotting scope is the only additional tool required. If you treasure the unusual, you will find the information about each species to be exhilarating.

Once smitten, you may decide you really can spare the time and energy required for the care and feeding of a geezer. With that in mind, you will also find a few live-capture techniques.

My hope is that each time you see an especially interesting geezer you will reach for this guide. Use the information confidently, yet wisely. Don't shy away.

WHAT EXACTLY IS A GEEZER?

According to Webster's Collegiate Dictionary, a geezer is: "A queer, odd, or eccentric man"–from the Scottish word "guiser," or one in disguise.

How would you define a geezer? Most people I asked hadn't given it a lot of thought. My son, himself a prospective member of the genus, called them "geeks gone gray," and "nerds gone gnarly." My mother replied "old reprobates." One lifelong observer offered, "They're nothing but an aberrant form of giant monkey! Have you noticed how some of them drag their knuckles when they walk?"

One former workmate swore up and down that he, by God, was not a geezer. He wiped the groundhog grease off his chin and described one as follows: "He's a guy with a gray stubble beard on his face; snoose on his teeth and running down his chin; a weather-beaten face from fishing in all kinds of weather and times of the day and night; and he's kind of half-baked, meaning he isn't all there. He's missing a couple of bricks and possibly teeth, and his dipstick hasn't registered full for quite some time." Alas, he had fallen prey to myths and stereotypical definitions of a geezer.

Nor do they have a reputation for great intelligence. However, I've observed that, depending on motivators provided, geezers are, in fact, in the same intellectual cage as other hominids. Another myth is that they all wear *eau de geezer*, that you can smell them before you see them. But this is not usually true.

Some observers think you must be retired to be a full-fledged member of the genus. Yet I've observed baby geezers still in their cribs. Others as young as forty can be seen wearing high-water pants, white socks, and suspenders *with* a belt. As much as anything, being a geezer is a state of mind.

Still others believe that members of this curious branch of hominids are closer to *Homo neanderthalensis,* that they merely fool us by walking upright.

Throughout history geezers have been depicted on stamps, coins and currency. In many ancient cultures, geezers enjoyed a special place of honor. Ancient Egyptians considered them to be "wise souls" and occasionally used their images to symbolize particular gods. Crude portraits of very old geezers have been used on crests to protect tribes against evil spirits. Flags with the faces of duffers have been used to lead armies into battle, protect them from danger, and scare the enemy.

This field guide is limited in that it identifies only the more common species of Caucasian geezers I've encountered in the contiguous United States. And while I've had the rare good fortune of observing a few costumed, dignified *uber* geezers in the alpine meadows of Austria and Switzerland, my research on that particular species is too preliminary to include.

COMMON TRAITS

There's no such thing as a generic geezer, although many share similar traits. For instance, most wear a hat or cap he rarely removes, a cap that makes a statement. This has contributed to the occurrence of reverse Mohawks, or balding, in an array of geezers. But you must remember this: removing his cap and misplacing it can cause impotence.

More oblivious members of the species will wear suspenders with clothes one might describe as "protective coloration," that is to say plaid pants and opposing plaid shirts—geezer camo—so they can more easily blend into their vintage furniture. To avoid detection, a few shy individuals will adopt clothing items with an actual camouflage pattern and wear them every day.

They will have names like Fritz, Howard, Hank, Ed, Norm, Bud, Woody, Augie, Jimmy, or just plain Dave.

When they're out and about, some of them have a constant companion—a very small dog, such as a miniature poodle, terrier or Chihuahua. You can often spot geezers shopping at thrift stores, flea markets or yard sales for clothing and collectibles, while their little dog waits patiently in the truck. The more adventurous members of the various species will seek treasures in dumpsters. A few carry cards that identify them as members of the Dumpster Divers of America.

Many clip coupons. Especially creative bachelors will save money by mending his clothes with needles crafted from cactus thorns, and making car repairs using duct tape. Money saved by being smart can be spent on geezer bling (small tools) and big-boy toys.

The waist band of many a geezer's pants can be found below his stomach, just above his magic parts. Still others wear their waist bands up under their armpits, with the aforementioned suspenders *and* a belt. For identification purposes, you can usually forget about looking at "rump patterns," because when you go to check out his buns, there won't be any.

During dinner one evening, one geezer companion repeatedly wiped his hands on his socks, instead of using the napkin. When I said, rather petulantly, "Did I just see you wipe your hand on your sock?" He replied, "Yep. I've done it all my life. Usually don't get caught. Lots of guys do it." Then he grabbed my hand and wiped it on *my* sock, and this felt quite natural.

Extroverted geezers are most animated and gregarious while having coffee with their peers. Every morning, at Tables of Wisdom in cafes across the country, they tell stories, share their whoopee-cushion wit, and discuss the news. Except when talking about fishing, they believe everything they say is true. The introverts among them will keep tattered, folded articles from newspapers in their billfolds to prove a point, knowing words might fail them.

Puttering is a beautiful way to fill time. The simplest task, like fixing a leaky faucet, can take days, and for several mornings at the Table of Wisdom he'll talk about the ins and outs of this five-minute project. While most geezers keep themselves constructively occupied, I did meet a few who don't actually *do* much of anything. They talk a lot about fixing their trucks, building a garage, patching a leaky roof, or going to Alaska. But these individuals often stop drinking coffee at noon, switch to beer and continue to talk about their pet projects.

Nearly all of them love old pickup trucks, and think of them as investments. Some can't have too many old cars or trucks in their yards to work on–someday. A favorite pastime is loitering around automobile graveyards in search of a part for one of their "classic" cars. They also hang out at used car lots kicking tires and getting salesmen's hopes up. When you're out driving around and see a small house with what looks like a junkyard or a debris recruitment program, you'll know you're in geezer habitat.

While driving down the highway, he will risk his life and yours by stopping suddenly to pick up an object on the road that is rusted and bent beyond recognition. He will leave his truck parked in the flow of traffic, ignore the honking horns, retrieve the thing, and say with glee, "Might be just what I need some time." At home he will add it to one of his debris piles. Later, when it is "just what he needs some time," he will not be able to find it.

He will affectionately name his favorite pickup, often an older Ford F-150, something like "Old Blue" or "Betsy." He might name it after a former sweetheart, one who never knew of her status as his girlfriend. If he lives in a rural northern climate, he won't invest in an engine block heater for his vehicle. On sub-zero days, he'll simply build a fire under it. While waiting for the fire to warm the engine, he will write yellow cuss words in the snow while urinating.

Retirees often travel abroad, play golf or restore antique cars, but the retired geezer will whittle or build small toys—tops that spin (from old wooden thread spools), "up-timiters" (to advise which way is up), or "round tuits" (as in "OK, dear. I'll get around to it.") Some are tech-savvy *entremanures* who sell their wares on Internet sites like Cafepress, Etsy, or eBay.

For many, horseshoes is the sport of choice, especially when forced to attend a family reunion.

If a geezer is really desperate to get out of household chores or shoveling snow, he will take up ice-fishing. He will don his finest winter plumage (layers of wool), and drive old Betsy right out onto the ice next to his peers. After augering holes in the ice with an oversized power drill and dropping in several lines, he'll stand around with his pals and mutter about how damn cold it is. Others with more sense, or who aren't such tightwads, will own their own ice shanties, complete with satellite TV. Some will simply take the bull by the horns and go to sleep late in the fall. If this happens, his mate will learn everything she needs to know about geezer hibernation.

He may get the newspaper from his mailbox or front porch wearing only his boxer shorts, secretly hoping someone will see him. Especially tough and brave geezers in the Great Lakes area do this in the middle of winter.

They do not hesitate to scratch where it itches.

Some are loners. They've made a healthy break from the crowd ethic, gathering with their peers only for coffee and ice fishing, although even these guys will tell you proudly that they belong to the local 4-H Club (because they have Hemorrhoids, Hernias, Hiccups and not much Hair).

They are usually forgiven almost anything, even the jokes they play on each other. But they can also harbor grudges for a very long time, preferably forever. Some would rather go to a proctologist than suffer a confrontation. Often he will remain single until he meets a woman evolved enough to understand his special needs.

A fellow geezer girl reports that when she's driving and her introverted geezer is riding shotgun, he will not yell, "Stop! You're about to run a red light!" Instead, he will clear his throat loudly. Over time, she has learned to listen for this acoustical signal that could save their lives.

After a few beers, a geezer might quote his favorite saying, such as "He's too smart by one-half," or "Sometimes I wake up grouchy; sometimes I let her sleep." Others predict the weather with the saying, "Little flakes big snow; big flakes, little snow." If you're around him much, these sayings will become extremely familiar, and you will smile (or cuss) to yourself every time you hear it.

Let's not neglect the economic importance of geezers. Who else would buy all that stuff with odd sayings printed on them, like baseball caps and shiny jackets embroidered with sayings like

OLD FART, or DOWN WITH UNDERWEAR? A Geezer Girl might wear a T-shirt that says MY NEXT HUSBAND WILL BE NORMAL. If he or she owns a working ranch in Montana, a jacket might say GINGER'S HERD BULLS. Others will have boats or license plates with identifying names like TIEAFLY or BLUE-BY-YOU. A bumper sticker might say something like: I'M NOT OLD, JUST MATURE, or HONK IF YOU LOVE GEEZERS, or THE WAY TO A FISHERMAN'S HEART IS THROUGH HIS FLY. One Great Lakes Geezer named Richard had a large vintage wood boat boldly emblazoned with the moniker BIG DICK.

He might carry a business card that says LICENSE TO HUG. Not exactly pinnacles of song complexity, they go about their tinkering while whistling tunes like "Put Your Little Foot." Favorite sing-a-longs include "North to Alaska." A retired truck driver might sing, "Give Me Forty Acres and I'll Turn This Rig Around."

Early morning vocalizations, such as throat-clearing and associated activities, can resemble sounds made by porcupines or other fauna fighting over food.

Geezers in general are known to pull some highly creative tricks on each other. One I heard about, who had cooked in logging camps in the North Idaho woods, put raisins in everything to cut down on complaints about flies in the food.

PART 2

GEEZER IDENTIFICATION –
the Field Notes and How to Use 'Em

Let's talk taxonomy. All humans, including geezers, fall into one big Family (an actual taxonomic term) that scientists call Hominids. We are members of a biological group who walk on two feet. Next we have Genus, which is a group of species exhibiting common characteristics (e.g. *Homo*) and Species *(sapiens)*, which means *modern man*. Early in my research I determined that the curious branch of Hominids called geezers deserved their own unique Genus: *Geezerus* and that each specific group would have his or her own Species *(e.g. Geezerus wader-en-sus)*.

Even though boundaries can be fuzzy, the trick to becoming a competent geezer gazer is to first determine what species you have at the other end of your binoculars. Then ask yourself: what are the odds of making such a sighting?

Both the **Common Name** (or names) and **Scientific Name** are given for each species. While the common name(s) may vary, for instance

Pelagic Geezer and Boating Geezer, you can count on the scientific name to remain the same *(Geezerus aqueous).* As previously suggested, this guide is limited to only the most popular or common species of old white duffers found in the contiguous U.S. Nor does it address the true vagrants that can occur in any scientific study of a genus. An example would be the rare sighting of a Sasquatch, or Bigfoot.

Under **Description**, you will find appearance and habits of dress, along with a few hints on behaviors commonly associated with the species.

The information included under **Habitat and Range** indicates whether one is aquatic (you are likely to find him on or near water), or terrestrial (usually seen on land). Some species, of course, are both aquatic *and* terrestrial. Many individuals are highly mobile and tolerate a variety of habitats, especially during seasonal migrations to warmer climates where the fishing is better and the leaverites are bigger.

A map of distribution is unnecessary. In addition to rural areas, geezers of every ilk can be found in the suburbs and rural fringes of the largest cities, even serving as mayors and populating state legislatures. Some states can brag that their governor is a member of the genus *Geezerus*. And in the past century, more than one president could be referred to as the Geezer-in-Chief.

I've identified a **Song** that members of each species might hum, whistle or sing as they go about their day and think no one is listening. Getting close enough to hear this song, however, can be tricky and may require stealth tactics. General vocalizations (e.g. other noises they might make) are covered elsewhere.

The **Comments** section gives you clues to the quirky behaviors displayed by members of a specific group.

When studying the Field Notes, you may notice that a few special geezers don't fit neatly into any category. They have made a healthy break from the crowd ethic while exhibiting multiple traits, such as the one guy I heard about who lives in an old motel. He hoards junk just like any duffer worth his salt. About once a year he cleans his place by shoving all loose belongings under the bed and blowing out his room with a leaf blower. I heard about him from a geezer who, at the time, lived on one of the San Juan Islands in a travel trailer. His neighbors made their homes in old school buses and shanties, all of them with successful debris recruitment programs. They called their dirt road The Street of Dreams.

When Geezers Change Zip Codes

FIELD NOTES

Common Name: Boating Geezer;
                  Pelagic Geezer

Scientific Name: *Geezerus aqueous*

Description: These   members   of   The
Rusty Zipper Club most often sport a T-shirts
and shorts, even in winter. Sometimes they will
have frost on their kneecaps. In summer they
trade in their tennies for flip-flops, ignoring the
mold between their toes. On evenings and week-
ends you will see members of this species working on their boats, in their back yards or at the
dock. You will hear Jimmy Buffet tunes. Once or
twice a season they will actually take the boat out
for a spin. Sometimes one will spend decades
building a sailboat in his garage, never asking
himself: will this boat go through the door when
I finally finish building it?

Habitat/Range: This group usually frequents
oceans, seashores, marinas, large inland lakes
and reservoirs, always in the company of a boat
powered either by an engine or the wind. When
not working on their boats, they can be found
wherever boat gear is sold. Occasionally, he will

wear a live parrot on his shoulder, like the one I met named Chicken of the Sea. Chicken's human claimed his parrot ate his transistor radio and the zipper slider right off his foul-weather parka. Others walk along the docks with a cat on a leash. For a dog, he or she might have a Portuguese Water Dog named Winslow Homer, or a yellow lab named Squid.

Song: "Cheeseburger in Paradise," by Jimmy Buffet (himself a *Geezerus aqueous*).

Comments: I overheard one guy brag about the sextant he constructed to navigate his sailboat on the ocean. He used copper tubing, a protractor, fishing line and a sinker. He was last heard from in the area of the Bermuda Triangle.

If he is also a nerd, he will outfit his boat with the latest gadgets including a toilet through which you could flush an overcoat, and he will brag about this loudly and often.

Most do not belong to yacht clubs, *per se*.

Both genders sometimes sail to warm climates to do sailing charters. A *G. aqueous* with both oars in the water will acquire (online or elsewhere) a ministerial certificate that allows him (or her) to legally perform weddings, funerals, and other odd ceremonies at sea.

One Pelagic Geezer told me a story he swore was true. "Yeah," he said." I built me a metal sailboat. Didn't put an engine in it. Me and another guy sailed it to Hawaii. We liked Hawaii so much we stayed quite a while. Sat there so long at anchor, watching sunsets come and go, that coral and other stuff grew thick on the bottom of the boat. When we finally sailed out of the cove through the gap in the reef, the fouled bottom slowed us down quite a lot. When the wind kicked up we were blown on top of the reef, where we sat like a teeter-totter. So we both ran forward to the bow at the same time, which caused the boat to slide off the reef into deep water on the other side of the cove. This scraped all the growees and coral leeches off the bottom and the boat sailed just fine after that."

How Geezers Came to America

FIELD NOTES

Common Name: Boreal
                 (or Spotted-Owl) Geezer

**Scientific
Name**:   Geezer*us boreal-us*

Description: A Boreal Geezer often wears
huge black boots in the brand of choice called
White boots, but when he stops at a bar after
work, he'll be wearing slippers. While some wear
blue jeans, always loosely and often with colorful
suspenders, others wear black high-water pants,
i.e. pants with the legs cut off above their ankles.
I once worked with a guy who only wore the
brand of black pants with the label *Wild Ass* on
the back pocket.

They don't go anywhere, especially to the woods,
without a very large thermos full of coffee. If you
are in a forest anywhere at 10:00 a. m. during
the week, you'll see their trucks screech to a halt.
They will reach for their thermos bottles, pour
coffee into the lids that serves as cups, and sit
looking out the windshield at the old growth. As
attached as they are to these thermos bottles,
however, they do not assign them pet names.

Habitat/Range: Within or very near forests stretching from Alaska to Newfoundland. When these guys aren't in the woods they're talking about the woods. After they retire, they can be found peeking out from the willows with Western Riverside Geezers, fishing the West. But their hearts are always in the woods. If you think you saw that elusive creature called *Bigfoot*, it was probably a Boreal Geezer.

Song: *Hoo, hoo-hoo, hoo-ah . . yee-yowuhhh. . hoo, hoo-hoo, hoo-ah yee-owuhhh*   (The call of the spotted owl.)

Comments: I once worked for the U. S. Forest Service, an agency that could brag, if it chose to, about its high Boreal Geezer population. At one Forest Service office, there were so many overly mature members of this species working that it became known throughout the region as The Jurassic National Forest. These guys do not *network*. When they return from headquarters, they say they were out *running their trap lines*. (A trap line is a route or circuit along which a series of animal traps is set.) If you ask who they saw, they will tell stories about the other members of *G. backwoods-i-us* they ran into at 10:00 a.m.

FIELD NOTES

Common Name: Cowboy Geezer

**Scientific
Name**:   *Geezerus
                     home-on-the-range-us*

Description: In addition to big, heavy belt
buckles that set off alarms at airport security
checkpoints, both authentic and pretend Cowboy
Geezers wear cowboy boots, blue jeans, shirts
with pearly snaps (instead of buttons), and bolo
ties. When they remove their boots at night you
will notice that their toes overlap, and their big
toes and little toes angle in toward each other.

Habitat/Range: They are truly home, home
on the range, and it's not the size of the spread
that counts. While driving along two-lane
highways in Montana, you can, if you're lucky,
still be stopped by a real cattle drive, complete
with Cowboy Geezers of all ages on horseback.
You must fight the urge to get out of the car and
help herd the cows. I've tried this. They do not
want your help.

Song: "Back in the Saddle Again,"
                             by Gene Autry

Comments: They like to make big bets
by saying little things like, "Bet you a nickel to a
sack of horse manure," and tend toward
comparisons like, "It was drier than a snake's
belly in a desert wagon track," "Crazier than a
shit-house rat," or "Scarce as rocking horse
poop."

Many utter the saying *Horse shit!!!* every damn
time they sneeze, and the signature vocalization
of such individuals will be recognized and com-
mented on all over town as well as out on the
range.

When a single *G. home-on-the-range-us* dons
his best hat and burp cloth (neckerchief) before
heading out the door to run *his* trap line, this
means he'll be making the rounds of the local
watering holes to visit with the late night Buckle
Bunnies.

FIELD NOTES

Common Name: Farmer Geezer;
                     Gentleman Farmer Geezer

Scientific Name: *Geezerus*
                     manure-on-the-boots-us

Description: Farmer Geezers wear over-
alls over flannel shirts in winter and T-shirts in
summer. They always wear baseball caps with
sayings like JOHN DEERE or HUCK'S FEED &
GRAIN. The sign on one Minnesota dairy
farmer's gate reads, ALL WE HAVE WE OWE
TO UDDERS.

Habitat/Range: Found on farms across
North America. They might be driving large
combines, backhoes and tractors, some with air-
conditioning and stereo systems. The more
evolved members of the species will listen to
opera while tending their fields. Many display
the rusted hulk of an antique Fordson tractor on
a mound in their front yards next to a windmill
replica, and house a restored 1020 International
tractor in a climate-controlled room in his barn.

A variety of this species, the Gentlemen Farmer Geezer, occupies five-acre farms, every square inch of which is put to good use. He lived in a city until he found his own bit of heaven, complete with a bovine or two.

His spread might be big but his range is typically small—from his house to the barn, barn to the field, field to tractor or combine, tractor or combine to the house, house to town to the hardware store, feed store, and local Table of Wisdom for coffee. Many of these guys will only take time away from their regular routine to attend antique steam engine and tractor shows. He might sport a T-shirt that says, *Manure Movers of America, Local 239*.

Song: "Old MacDonald
                            Had a Farm"

Comments: One member of *G. manure-on-the-boots-us* I met proudly reported that at a dress-up affair he put the ashes from his roll-your-own cigarette in the cuff of his dress-up pants, which, at the time, was convenient. His pants caught fire but luckily he tore them off right away. Other than getting an awful lot of attention, no harm was done.

By the nature of their profession, they never retire. A few chew tobacco, which dribbles down their chins as they discuss the weather or the good old days, or listen to radio updates about Russian wheat aphids and the price of hogs. In the winter, all of them watch "tractor porn," i.e. look at pages of tractor parts or watch old tractors racing on Youtube. com.

FIELD NOTES

Common Name: Gearhead Geezer

Scientific Name: *Geezerus gears-R-us*

Description: This steadfast species wears practical clothes, such as black denim pants and dark plaids that don't easily show dirt or grease. This alleviates the dilemma of deciding what to change into after his weekly shower. He doesn't comb his hair, if he has any, and he often wears the same baseball cap for years. If you can get him to a movie theater he will refuse to remove his cap, and once back home he'll wear it to bed if you let him. To save time and money on grooming, many grow beards along with ear and nose hairs long enough to wrap a package. They are retired machinists, tool and die makers, mechanics, even mechanical engineers.

Habitat/Range: Their work is never done and it is carried out in shops, garages, and basements across North America. They inhabit those places the rest of us call "man caves," leaving these lairs to eat, sleep, meet their peers at the local Table of Wisdom, and attend car and motorcycle swaps, antique tractor and steam engine shows, farm and equipment auctions, and garage sales.

Many members of *G. gears-R-us* prefer to live in the country, where they can accumulate treasures without interference from civilization and those pesky covenants. But if they live in towns, their back yards and alley ways can be cluttered with projects awaiting restoration: rusted pieces of equipment like brake drums, axles, and drive shafts, along with a vintage boat that leaks, and often an old International pickup truck he will call *Cornbinder*. While these guys are mechanical geniuses when it comes to pet projects, their lawn mowers usually haven't run in years, partly because it's impossible to cut the grass with all those rusted hunks of metal hiding there.

Song: "One Piece at a Time"
                        by Johnny Cash

Comments: Empirical research shows that this species is directly descended from the hominids who invented the wheel. While the species truly has evolved since then, in certain areas of their brains they can seem to have gears instead of gray matter. They deal only in predictability, absolutes, and logic.

Instead of reading a large-print book, he will reach for his always handy geeky lookers—those eyeglass magnifiers with a headband used for quality control inspection. I know one who files his nails with a belt sander and uses a rotary Dremel tool to remove calluses on his feet. Yet another guy invented an air freshener with an old car smell. But if you ask one what the term *quantum mechanics or quantum physics* means, he will scratch his whiskers thoughtfully. If you mention *the law of attraction,* he will point to the debris recruitment program in his back yard. If you suggest that he appears to practice *wabi sabi* (the ancient Oriental notion of appreciating the beauty of imperfection and impermanence), he won't have a clue what you're talking about.

While most of us blubber about some devastating loss, they will appear stoic and unemotional, until it comes to losing a heart throb such as an old hood ornament from an early 1950s Pontiac or Oldsmobile. He will say, "In case you didn't notice, that's a piece of sculpture with a unique personality." Signs that he is mourning its loss include pulling his baseball cap low on his forehead, withdrawing his neck into his plaid shirt, and hiding in his man cave for days if not weeks.

FIELD NOTES

Common Name: Metro Geezer

**Scientific
Name**:   *Geezerus glam-o-rus*

Description: At first glance, you might
mistake a *G. glam-o-rus* for a Geezer Girl, but if
you look at body conformation the difference
soon becomes apparent. Their hairdos tend to be
longish and, like their cousins the Ponytail
Geezers, many sport little gray ponytails. But
they tend to vary from the other species by
wearing Gucci accessories and at least one
earring.

These highly creative individuals are the butter-
flies of the geezer world, thanks to their colorful
dress and high attractiveness quotient. They are
not afraid to wear pink (or mango or peach), and
often wear silk underwear or vintage tap panties
under their dress slacks or kilts. A few of them
hide wigs and dresses in their closets and play
dress-up when they're alone, or at special
conventions. Their fingernails are always mani-
cured, and they get pedicures for their frequent-
flyer trips to the Caribbean. They view these

inclinations as opportunities, and pay top dollar for a hairstyle that complements their status as a "sensitive new age guy," aka a SNAG. Some even wear those kooky Five-finger Shoes. They might be retired hairdressers, interior designers, or high-ranking military officials. One time a character on the TV show *West Wing* announced that one in forty U. S. Presidents had roamed the halls of the White House wearing a prom dress.

Habitat/Range: They frequent cities with book stores and Starbucks coffee shops, where they can drink lattes and work on their unfinished screenplays. This species shows great plasticity in their choice of wintering sites, and have a strong fidelity for the more expensive Caribbean Islands. Many also live part of the year somewhere in Europe.

Songs: "A Guy is a Guy," Doris Day.

Comments: When you see him, the fol-lowing words might pop into your head: ex-travagant, theatrical, colorful, dashing, flashy, glamorous, ostentatious, resplendent, showy, swashbuckling and sensitive. A real member of this species cries openly with you at the movies. He will use the term *per se,* and know that it does not mean an expensive bag carried by a French prostitute.

This group holds the distinction of being the only *Geezerus* species who might claim to be a monk or mystic. Not only do these guys understand quantum physics, they subscribe to the law of attraction and practice *wabi sabi*. When you're in the presence of a bona fide G. *glam-o-rus* there will be no doubt in your mind which species he belongs to.

FIELD NOTES

**Common
Name**:   North Woods or Great Lakes
                 Geezer, alias The Minnesota
                 Iceman

**Scientific
Name**:   *Geezerus frigid-us*

Description: This species was made fa-
mous by the movie, *Grumpy Old Men*. They tend
to wear wool year round, often plaids, and those
sensible Elmer Fudd hats with the ear flaps.

Habitat/Range: They occur mostly in Wisconsin, Minnesota and in that separate country,
the Upper Peninsula of Northern Michigan.

Song: "The Cry of the Wild Goose,"
                      by Frankie Laine

Comments: While members of most species are perfectly happy with a modest second
home, like a camper on their old F-150 Ford
truck or vintage International pickup, these guys
prefer elaborate hunting shacks and ice fishing
shanties. Many are outfitted with a recliner and a

satellite TV, and they never invite their wives to these lairs. Maybe his ice shanty is one of several in the area, because it can take a village to catch a big fish. As the days grow longer, they sit around the ice holes on lawn chairs drinking beer and freezing their hinders while waiting for the fish to bite. A popular topic of discussion is when to get the heck off the ice before it melts right out from under them.

An especially classy member of *G. frigid-us* will install a urinal on the side of a tree near his hunting shack.

Some of these guys like to catch fish called Northern pikes. One of them told me, "Yeah, sure. I like to pickle my Northerns."

Geezer Hunting Camp

FIELD NOTES

Common Name: Old Geezer Miner

Scientific Name: *Geezerus find-the-gold-us*

Description: Old Geezer Miners dress a lot like Boreal Geezers, but tend to wear rubber gumboots and red suspenders to hold up their black twill pants. Instead of a baseball cap, he sometimes sports a felt fedora like Jimmy Stewart wore in the Alfred Hitchcock film, "Vertigo" or like the gangsters wore in the 1920s and 30s.

Habitat/Range: They hang out at shows where rocks are displayed. Sometimes they frequent the taverns (edge habitat) near rivers, where they drink beer and fish alongside their pals, the Western Riverside and Lakeshore Geezers. Some have active mining claims on national forest land and make the required improvements on the claim each year in hopes of finding a vein and striking it rich. You can spot them panning for gold at stream's edge in areas near ghost towns where a gold rush once occurred. During winter months, these same geezers are stooped over in the desert picking up rocks that normal people wouldn't notice, rocks called *leaverites* (leave 'er right where you found 'er).

Song: "Heart of Gold,"Neil Young

Comments: Some *G. find-the-gold-us* own elaborate equipment to cut and polish their leaverites for making jewelry, including bolo ties. When they go for coffee, their pockets bulge with rock specimens, artifacts, and samples of their latest wares.

They tend to say things like "tap 'er light" instead of "goodbye, *ciao*, or *hasta la vista*." Tap 'er light does not mean "leave some beer in the keg for me." It means "Don't tap the dynamite powder into the drill hole so hard that you blow yourself up." This term is especially familiar to geezers called "powder monkeys," who use dynamite in their work.

In the north, certain ice fishermen keep bait from freezing by placing it between their lower lip and gum, which works especially well with maggots. The word is that only old retired miners from Butte, Montana, can "geezer up" sufficiently to lip-warm their bait.

FIELD NOTES

Common Name: Ponytail Geezer;
Beach Boys Geezer

**Scientific
Name**:

*Geezerus
a-man-named-Sue-us*

Description: He, too, will someday lose his hair, but for now he has sufficient gray hairs to wear a ponytail. This statement of independence and freedom might be only a pigtail, or it might be big and bushy like a squirrel's tail. Many have a diverse wardrobe and dress up—or down—for special occasions. He might delight in carrying an old military ALICE (All Purpose Individual Carrying Equipment) pack, which can become permanently attached to his armpit. Like other species, they develop long-term relationships with their baseball caps. He might also sport a tattoo.

Habitat/Range: A migrating species, *G. a-man-named-Sue-us* is found throughout North America. And if you are a world traveler, watch for them wherever ex-pats flock in winter. Unlike their cousins, the Silver-Crowned Geezer, this is a non-fishing group, although they can be both terrestrial and aquatic. If you're particularly observant, you can still occasionally spot one surfing. They also range wherever motorcycles go, sometimes migrating in flocks to and from Sturgis, South Dakota.

Song: "Yesterday When I was
                             Young," by Roy Clark"

Comments: When finally free to do so, both retired corporate executives and military personnel tend to let down their hair.

Some have studios where they weld sculptures from old car and motorcycle parts. Others make necklaces from trade beads. Especially creative members of this species use chainsaws to carve large wood *objets d'art*. Still others play the guitar, always amplified, and start bands like "The Trust Fund Hippies." They will forever remain committed to the songs of the 1970s.

While their range is global, their numbers are limited. There was only one 1960s-1970s era, during which most of them came of age. And many are veterans. For these reasons, they are considered   a   special   population   on   the

threatened and endangered species list and must
be treated with understanding and respect.

FIELD NOTES

Common Name: Renaissance Geezer

Scientific Name: *Geezerus mensa-candidat-us*

Description: Benjamin Franklin was intellectually curious, charismatic, mentally adroit, larger than life, grandiloquent and rhetorical, yet he walked around with his shoes untied. Like all Renaissance Geezers, he was enlightened. Pay no attention to dress; listen, instead, to their voices.

Habitat/Range: No doubt there were members of this fascinating species among the Neanderthals. Today they can be found in the smallest towns and the largest cities, in the open country, and on islands no bigger than shopping malls. At Tables of Wisdom he will be the alpha geezer, the one who talks loudest and most while using words with numerous syllables.

Song: "I'll Do It My Way,"
by Frank Sinatra

Comments: Renaissance Geezers are incredibly versatile. Handy to have around, they can build or fix anything. Some are so smart they not only read the instruction manuals, they understand and follow them. They know just enough about most things to sound like an expert on any topic, whether it be Medieval history or current events. Sometimes while listening to one talk, your jaw will drop. You may ask yourself, "How does he know precisely why the sky is blue when I never even thought to ask the question?"

Politically, these individuals are often neither to the right nor the left but will vote Independent, Green Party or Libertarian. He will say, "I'm no radical. I merely pay attention to what's *really* going on. My vote depends entirely on the facts and who would do the best job."

This curious species is able to talk in double negatives if he finds himself in the presence of someone who does this. He wants to bond with others, to show empathy. Or maybe it's an opportunity to be his authentic self. His own father and both grandfathers were probably less evolved. He may be only one generation away from ice fishing in winter, hunting the turnouts on back roads, or working with manure on his boots.

While most geezers who survive a hellish event might say, "Yeah, it was a real goat rope – a helluva *debuckle*," a Renaissance Geezer not only knows exactly what a *debacle* is but also how to properly say and spell it.

If the words *astute, brilliant, verbose* or even *know-it-all* come to mind, you are in the presence of a *G. mensa-candidat-us*.

How a Geezer Discovered Electricity

FIELD NOTES

Common Name: Silver-Crowned Geezer;
California Gray-Crowned
Geezer; Geezer Emeritus

Scientific Name: Geezer*us been-a-round-us*

Description: If not yet retired, a member of this species might be disguised in a three-piece suit, heading up a very large organization, a department at a large university, or a natural history museum. If he is retired, he's the one writing his memoirs or a book of essays while wearing a canvas vest with eighteen pockets. A highly trained dog lies at his feet, a dog he drove into Canada or across the U. S. to buy, one that retrieves dead ducks. He might own a ranch in Montana with a river running through it. This is one of the few species you will never find diving in a dumpster for treasures. A few proudly sport "reverse Mohawks," or if mostly bald, will shave off his remaining hair to make a statement.

Habitat/Range: The pastime of fly-fishing and the high economic status of the species allow these beguiling geezers to occupy a greater range of habitat than most. During their frequent migrations, they fish streams in New Zealand Scotland, Iceland, Argentina, or Montana.

Song: "The Good Life,"
                             by Tony Bennett

Comments: While some people believe
this species to be the most evolved of all, others
consider them to be pseudo-geezers. After all,
authentic members of this genus don't take vaca-
tions to fish — they *live* to fish. However, while
it's true that many own and drive sports cars or
fly their own small jets, when they're in geezer
mode they, too, drive old pickup trucks.

One time I encountered a Geezer Emeritus fly
fishing the Ruby River in Montana. A college
professor, he talked about getting his fishing line
tangled in "that riparian vegetation" down by the
riverside. Often eccentric, they like to say things
like "qualitatively quantify" and "cobble gravel
substrate." However, in a heart-to-heart discussion he might spout something like, "If there's
any more visceral to get out, let's hear it."

One *G. been-around-us* named Augie got his
name when his father made a bet while playing
poker. If he lost the game, he had to name his
first-born after the other guy--a man named
August

FIELD NOTES

Common Name: Techno Geezer;
                               #Hashtag Geezer

Scientific Name: Geezer*us tech-ni-cus*

Description: Most geezers understand the words "instant-messaging" to mean burping loudly following a good meal. However, this method of sending and receiving notes electronically was actually invented by a Techno Geezer. Until the 1990s these guys were called nerds. But then they shed their plastic pocket protectors in favor of the latest computer and other electronic doodads, or they invented their own. And since no one would go out with them, they had a little extra money to invest in tech stocks. Members of this species were overjoyed with their new toys, and started their own computer companies to keep out of jail for hacking. They usually wear jeans and a T-shirt, but will dress up for a big meeting by throwing on an un-ironed cotton thrift store shirt.

Habitat/Range: They are found wherever electronic gear is sold (or designed and manufactured). Young geezers-in-training work at these venues, while those who have already reached the status of *G. tech-ni-cus* own them. Other favorite haunts include hardware stores, computer shops, and chandleries that sell the latest sailboat gadgetry. Most are so *green* and *cool* they don't even have mailboxes, except on their electronic devices.

Occasionally one will hunt or fish, mostly so he can research and buy things like night vision goggles and sonar fish finders. He will download a smart phone app to use with an amplifier in order to bugle for elk, but when the herd of elk arrives he will not remember where he left his gun.

Song: "High Geared Daddy,"
                              by Webb Pierce

Comments: This guy is definitely in "The Cloud." Not only does he always carry a smart phone, he uses the built-in personal assistant to help run his business. If he takes up running or race-walking, he'll buy a heart monitor and strap it to his chest. This gadget will record his mileage, time and heart rate. He will figure out how to get his heart monitor to talk to his computer or phone, and over the weeks he'll track his progress on an electronic spreadsheet. While members of other species still use the Grunt and Point System, which does not include stopping to ask directions, *G. tech-ni-cus* owns the latest Global Positioning System (GPS). Because he sometimes travels to remote areas, his phone is tuned in to satellites so he has access to his tech stocks. As a hobby, he likes to keep abreast of the latest espionage technology.

Many enjoy inventing things unrelated to computers. To keep raccoons from coming into his house, one acquaintance added a paw-recognition feature to his cat door so only his cat could enter. Another guy invented a tiny weed-whacker with which to trim his beard.

Members of *G. tech-ni-cus* are among the world's most affluent geezer species. Some of these geeks gone gray are even richer than their cousins and uncles, the Silver-Crowned Geezers.

FIELD NOTES

Common Name: Western Riverside
                  and Lakeshore Geezer

**Scientific
Name**:   <u>Fly fishing sub-species:</u>
                   G. *catch-and-release-us*
                   <u>Spin fishing sub-species:</u> .
                   G. *catch-and-filet-us*

Description: Although they tend to dress
like homeless people, their attire is usually acces-
sorized with a pair of waders if they're fly fishing,
or wet and muddy boots if they're spin casting
from the bank. Members of the latter sub-species
often sport a duct tape designer label and spray
their zippers with WD-40. They wear bucket hats
with all sorts of fishhooks and lures in them, and
sometimes matchsticks and toothpicks. Smart
ones include a bobber or two so that when the
wind blows his hat off while he's out on the lake,
it will float. Just like their cousins, the Silver-
Crowned Geezers, both sub-species wear fishing
vests with eighteen pockets plus loops and Velcro
pads, but these guys carry things like a plastic
whistle, flies or lures, and beef jerky or pieces of
fish they smoked in an old refrigerator. Their

vests look and smell as if they've housed more than one dead fish.

Habitat/Range: The states of Idaho, Montana, Washington, Oregon, and northwest Wyoming are areas of unusual species richness. In May, migratory restlessness sets in and geezers from elsewhere drive like bats out of hell as they flock toward Yellowstone country—not to watch geysers, but to fish. This is one of the few times they exhibit Type A behavior.

You will find this species wherever a fishable stream or lake occurs, whether it meanders through a sagebrush-covered meadow or tumbles down out of a coniferous forest. Bodies of water accessed by dirt roads leading to the water's edge qualify as habitat. If he can drive to his favorite fishing spot, this cuts down on the wear and tear on his waders. During fishing season, his wife often gets scarcely more than a glimpse of him after dark at the dinner table in the camper. Or, as she beats the bushes while calling his name, she may find his tracks next to the bank.

Song: "On the Road Again," by Willie Nelson

Comments: A member of this species was unearthed from two-million-year-old lake sediment in Oregon, still holding a fishing pole fashioned from a bone. There's speculation in unscientific communities that every Western Riverside and Lakeshore Geezer evolved from this one specimen.

Edge Habitat

During the off-season, or any time the fish aren't biting, a few members of *G. catch-and-release-us* collect Western art, while *G. catch-and-filet-us* might nap their afternoons away in front of the TV, waking up instantly if you try to change the channel from a football game, Texas wrestling, or "Fishing the West." One geezer reported that over the Christmas holidays he found himself gazing longingly at the aquarium next to the TV, wondering if he could successfully filet an angel fish.

During fishing season, this important species may seem shy, but they're only preoccupied. And they are not without charisma. They are, after all, fully accustomed to getting hot action out of cold fish.

FIELD NOTES

Common Name: White-Rumped Geezer

Scientific Name: Geezer*us buns-R-us*

Description: Heavier-bodied than other species, he actually has buns *and* wears his waist band low so that when he squats to change a tire, sort through a box of hats at a yard sale, or sit on a bar stool he will flash you a vertical smile. When you leave the scene, you will not remember what kind of clothes he was wearing.

Habitat/Range: The range of this endearing group is wide. You will catch sight of bare hinders across North America, both inland and on or near water, especially around boats and old cars that need fixing.

Song: "Blue Moon" as performed
                        by The Marcels

Comments: Members of this species could benefit from the Boating Geezer's all-purpose solution to problems, what they use instead of duct tape: Capt'n Tolly's Crack Cure.

In a genus that exhibits a high rate of obliviousness, these guys win the prize. He can become so preoccupied with the task at hand that he is unmindful that he is mooning us. Psychologists might tell us that he is, in fact, aware, that this act of exhibitionism has a purpose only his inner geezer knows. Summer evenings, he might scratch his head in wonderment and surprise when he discovers that his hinder is sunburned and riddled with mosquito bites. This scenario will repeat itself in winter when he realizes he has suffered freezer burn on his backside. One guy's wife told me she was going to pay for a tattoo on one of her geezer's cheeks that said, "What ya lookin' at?"

This easy-going species is not fussy about cuisine or couture, or whether you shave your legs. *G. buns-R-us* can be the easiest and most entertaining, whimsical, kind and generous of all mates.

FIELD NOTES

Common Name: Geezerette , Geezer Girl,
                   She-Geezer, Raging Granny

Scientific Name: Geezer*us fem-in-ist*

Description: Geezer Girls often sport an
hourglass shape. But just like any species, they
come in all shapes and sizes. Her hair is usually
cropped short in a no-nonsense style, and she's
proud of being a member of the "silver tsunami,"
refusing to use hair coloring. Some clever geezerettes cut their own hair with a Flowbee, an
electric-powered vacuum cleaner attachment
made for the purpose. They do not follow fashion
trends in a sheep-like manner and often wear
jeans, a T-shirt, boots, and a baseball cap.

Instead of wearing the waist of her jeans below
her navel, as is currently the style, she continues
to wear it at her natural waistline or even closer
to her armpits. Some of these darlings drove a
truck for a living, or maybe still do, and their
personal rig is usually a four-wheel drive pickup
or SUV. These women are highly independent,
and many have a very short banding history–

some of us several times. These girls steadfastly refuse to wear makeup or go on diets. They are among the most capable yet the kindest, most generous-spirited individuals I have ever met. Each is exceptionally beautiful in her own way.

Habitat/Range: Usually found in terrestrial areas, but they go wherever they darn well please. Many hunt and fish, and are highly skilled at gutting, cleaning, and cooking the catch (or kill) of the day. They attend (and sometimes perform at) cowboy poetry events, and they like pretty rocks and gems as much as the next geezer. Some even think tractors are sexy and follow Antique Tractor Shows as well as harmonica festivals.

Song: "I Don't Do Floors,"
                      written by Don Cook &
                      Charles Victor Rains, as
                      performed by Nikki Nelson.

Comments: Most members of *G. fem-in-ist* do occasionally seek out male members of the genus, although some don't give a hoot about the opposite sex. Those who *are* married are experts on their particular captive specimens and will happily share their observations.

Just like male members of the genus, these women had a lot of chores to do when they were children, and they walked long distances to and from school. You can hear them say, "You might think eight miles is a long way to walk, but we never thought a thing of it—we just put on our big-girl panties and we *did* it." You might have spoken this line yourself.

More sophisticated she-geezers wear purple outfits and red hats when they gather for cruises and other fun adventures. One small group I met on the island of St. John in the U.S. Virgin Islands calls themselves The Bridge Club. They don't play bridge, but instead do the following: build bridges, burn 'em, then take a cruise. Some of these women also belong to a group called The Middle-Aged Majorettes, who march in parades. The Drill Team in Southwest Utah marches in parades toting drills held high like torches. One pal of mine is a long-standing member of The Saddlebags, a group that meets to ride across entire western states. Others are proud members of Great Old Broads for Wilderness and the grassroots group of grannies who call themselves the Growing Brainless Together Club (GBTC).

Cowgirls and former rodeo queens are proud to be called Buckle Bunnies, and are unafraid to grace barstools at watering holes throughout the West. One particularly sassy cowgirl I know earns a living by brokering horse semen.

French geezer girls living in New York City (and there are quite a few), are called *Bag-ettes*.

Several beautiful geezer girls in Wisconsin sing *acapella* in a group called the Cheddar Chicks. A group of women in the Northwestern U.S. who compete in lumberjack contests call themselves The Chesty Choppers. And there are all those tough cookies in roller derby groups, many of them geezer girls in training.

More than a few members of *G. fem-in-ist* determine what to cook for dinner by checking to see how much room is left in the dishwasher.

Geezer Girls have a certain attitude about aging. Instead of whining that we don't have a sex life, we brag that we are *born-again virgins*. Neither do we say we're in our sixties. No sir, ma'am. We like to brag that we are actually $59.95 plus shipping and handling.

One woman told me her grandmother played poker with her breasts flopped up on the table to distract the other players.

My friend from "The Street of Dreams" gave me a list of positive attributes for the kind of geezerette he's looking for. She is: 1) low maintenance; 2) can gut a fish; 3) lets her geezer have his own "space," one she never enters; and 4) sees cultural value in the Canadian TV show "Trailer Park Boys."

PART 3

VIEWING TECHNIQUES

Before heading out the door, peruse the section called Field Notes regarding the habitats specific to the species you are stalking. Also review identification clues for silhouette and dress. Here are a few tips to consider.

Unless you like ice fishing, the best viewing opportunities occur in late spring, summer and fall, when geezers are moving about the countryside a great deal.

Except when stalking the few species that hang out in big cities, avoid wearing fluorescent clothing or other contemporary colors. Instead, dress to blend with the surroundings like they do.

Pay close attention to edge habitats near rivers and lakes. Cafes and taverns in these locations are prime watering holes. Once you find a geezer-rich area, make use of natural hiding cover, like bushes and tall grasses. Simply hide and watch, and be patient. If he senses your presence he might stop what he's doing, but if you have become part of the scenery he will soon resume his activity. If one of your body parts goes to sleep, remember to move very cautiously when attempting to restore feeling. Also, never point, laugh or wave your arms, and always watch where you put your feet. A snapping twig might alarm him and you might be put to work netting or cleaning a fish, or handing him a tool.

One woman reported trying various methods of calling geezers in closer. She made smooching noises without much success because the fish were biting that day. She had better luck yelling, "Ice cold beer! Over here! Ice cold beer!"

As you search for the more elusive species, you will meet others on the same quest. Compare notes. Ask questions. Most will share the thrill of discovery and their knowledge with you. Do not be intimidated by others with more experience. Remember, they, too, were once beginners. Top-notch geezer gazers love to show off their skills.

Remember, what a geezer does and why he does it are two different things, so resist the temptation of attributing motivation to their behavior.

PART 4

LIVE-TRAPPING YOUR OWN
— THE RULES
or GEEZERS AS PREY

For some, identifying and listing the various species provides sufficient satisfaction. Others wish to pursue members of a particular group and learn more about their lives. If you get hooked and ultimately decide you want one of your very own, here are a few things to consider.

Why Geezers Make Good Mates

- Each one is unique. This can be an important factor for those of us addicted to novelty and also subscribe to the belief that "normal" is overrated.

- While captive management of some geezers is problematic due to their migratory restlessness, most have a high nest-site fidelity.

- They can be good providers, if you like fish and wild game. Members of a few species are quite rich.

<u>Some Cautionary Facts:</u>

- Each geezer is unique. A generous anthropologist might say they are *idiosyncratic*.

- They are not avid fans of obedience training and don't always come when called. This doesn't mean they're stupid. They are quite smart about things they deem important.

- Most do not do well in confined spaces. They require considerable room to move around in, preferably out in the country where they can keep old cars and trucks, a shop or basement to hide and tinker in, and vegetation so they can take a leak outdoors. They don't last long in apartments.

- You may have a career of your own, but once you decide to take on a geezer you will need to become a homemaker.

- Many don't talk much, especially to women. They aren't into cuddling, either, but most allow touching late at night. Too much handling can be quite stressful to some individuals and cause them to suffer the dreaded "over-stimulation syndrome.

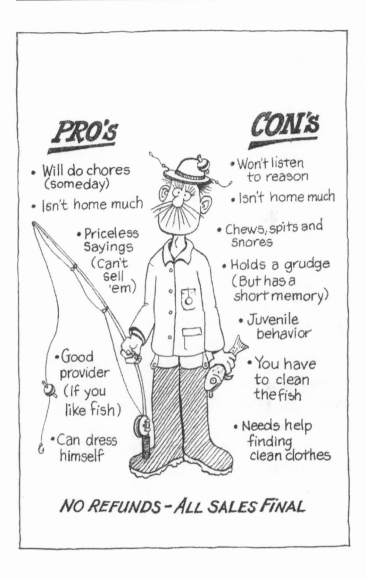

MEETING YOUR DREAM GEEZER

Once you make up your mind that you could love a geezer and grow old with him, your challenge is to choose carefully. Unfortunately, there is neither a 900-number nor a dial-a-geezer program. This makes it difficult to develop the communication skills you'll need before encountering an authentic specimen in the wild. Nor is there a rent-a-geezer business so you can "try before you buy."

But how exactly do you meet one? You could practice the law of attraction: repeatedly picture your dream geezer, and believe that someday you will find him. A complementary method is to sign up with a free Internet dating site like www.plentyoffish com. Or you can go out on a limb—all the way to the skinny branches—and put an ad on Craigslist. Whatever you do, don't be overly modest or timid when crafting your profile. Sit up straight and be bold. For if you can be open-minded, you might just net your very own "catch of the day."

A solo geezer sometimes occupies himself during the off-season by answering such ads if, based on the wording of your profile, there's a remote possibility you don't talk much, especially about your feelings.

First you must decide if you want one who is more likely to hang out on or near the water (aquatic) or on land (terrestrial). Terrestrial geezers are, as a general rule, not as skittish as aquatic species and often adapt well to captivity, especially if they're allowed to escape to a hunting camp each fall and an ice shanty each winter.

Aquatic geezers, on the other hand, have been known to drag anchor in an effort to escape a banding attempt for fear it will interfere with their lifestyle. They have bigger fish to fry than you, Babe. Ask yourself: do you even like boating? If so, do you like heavy weather, including thunder and lightning, wind, and house-sized waves? How strong *are* your boundaries? For instance, can you say "No!" loudly and often, when asked to clean a fish or the boat toilet, or steer the boat into a storm? Could you also say "Yes, Dear" as you hand him the right tool when he's working on the boat (even though you're busy in the tiny boat kitchen)? If you answer yes to both questions, they'll be all over you like a seagull on a June bug.

Or maybe you'd appreciate a member of a cross-over species who enjoys both land and water. They may offer the best (and worst) qualities of both. The bottom line: approach each one as an individual.

Don't be hasty. It's important not to choose based entirely on looks and body conformation. Also, since many of them require special conditions or care in order to be happy, you need to spend time with him to determine if you're up to the task.

Killing Time 'Til Fishing Season

Once you've met a prospective mate and arranged a meeting, remember your behavior must be carefully planned. Be sure to meet him on neutral territory. If sparks do fly, you can follow up on a second or third date by inviting him to your home for dinner. Courtship feeding is a good way to learn more about him. During dinner, does he reach down repeatedly to use his sock as a napkin? Does he wolf down his food as if he hasn't eaten in a week? Does he slurp his soup? Does he burp loudly and then smile? Does he have all of his teeth? Does any of this matter?

While courting, try talking about a subject that is sure to be of interest. Remember, diesel fumes are like pheromones to many geezers. Ask if he's thought of hopping a freighter across the Atlantic to watch and video record the engines operating. Having done your research, you already know that he would clip coupons and eat day old bread for the rest of his life to pay for such a trip, and that once back home he would view this recording over and over. Pay attention. When talking about this subject, does he become animated? Does his pulse visibly quicken? Do his pupils enlarge? If so, you will be able to get quite close.

One sure-fire way to capture the imagination of a Western Riverside or Lakeshore Geezer is to wear fishing lure earrings. I've seen earrings with names like Midnight Nibbler, designed for "quick and painless catch and release." Another model, the Mate Bait, is guaranteed to "land a real keeper," the kind even your mother would appreciate." I met a geezer girl on Whidbey Island, Washington, with a business named *Rust Revival*. She crafts surprisingly elegant earrings, called "Beerings," using old beer bottle caps.

When you finally come across a geezer of special interest, the first thing to do is to check out his banding history. Once you've determined he is, indeed, both single and not adverse to wearing a wedding band, then what? As you chat, his behavior will soon tell you if he's available for the intense level of observation required for you to decide if this one is a keeper.

Stop and think about his age. What age should your dream geezer be and does it make a difference? If you acquire one who is considerably older and has been single a long time, you may find that he'll have major adjustment problems.

If you're considering several different available geezers at the same time, here are some things you should look for when making your comparisons. First, is he bright and alert? Second, does he pull his head down into his neck? This might only indicate shyness. Just be quiet and wait until he extends his head again. Check his eyes. If they're shut and he refuses to open them, avoid that one. If his eyes are open, make sure they're clear and bright. Next inspect his nostrils and ears. Remember, hairs longer than normal can be trimmed away during routine grooming.

Alas, after exhausting every avenue and you still fail to meet and claim a desirable geezer of your very own, you might be a candidate for a life-sized duffer doll. Remember, it is completely honorable to live and shop *green*.

OPERATOR'S MANUAL or
HOW TO PRESERVE YOUR GEEZER

Feed him lots of tofu. Be sure to camouflage the tofu in a casserole, as most would rather eat a maggot than tofu. This advice comes with a very strong warning you must follow without fail: never tell his friends he eats tofu.

Remember, a happy geezer will have an attitude—good or bad. He'll express a certain *joie de vivre* and sass, even when grumpy. Every now and then, evaluate his mental health. A lethargic geezer is a sign that something is terribly wrong. But before you call a doctor, try increasing the amount of fiber in his diet and see if he perks up after a few days.

DO GEEZERS FACE EXTINCTION?

Never!

No special legislation will ever be necessary to protect this genus from extinction for one simple reason: a woman doesn't discover she's married to a member of the genus *Geezerus* until long after she has mated with him and heard the pitter-patter of additional waders. Once this has happened, she'll either learn to enjoy the fact that her husband is *different* or she will become very tolerant. This single truth guarantees the survival and further evolution of the curious branch of hominids called geezers.

ACKNOWLEDGMENTS

The idea for this guide was born over a campfire near Yellowstone National Park in the company of geezers. We were talking about how Europeans who visit Yellowstone National Park say *geezers* when they really mean *geysers*. We all knew them as the old duffers who spend summers fishing around Yellowstone, and that included a few of us—both male and female.

The more prominent geezers and geezerettes who inspired me in my research include Guy Hanson, Gordon Gray, Fred Dalbec, Jeff Parker, Ed Bauer, Jim Guest, Chuck Neal, Doug Reeves, Betsy Jagger, Dusty Dunbar, Dick Lamuth, and Rel and Jackie Looney. Special thanks for encouragement and ideas go to Kathryn Hamshar, Rosemary Hamshar, Penny Bews, and Sherry Gohr. My dear old dad, Wesley Moore, alias Post Hole Augerson, set the high standard by which I measure all geezers. Thanks also to Kenton Allen for his quirky ideas. Gifted artist, John A. Alley, developed and drew the illustrations with a perfect blend of skill and humor. Jennifer Rod helped with illustrations, during the years John was hiding from me in Nebraska.

Valuable editorial advice shaped this book. Thanks go to Mary Lu Perham, Scott Brown and wildlife biologists Cary Derringer and Jodie Canfield. Heartfelt gratitude goes out to Carol (Gotcher) Wallace, who was in on this project from the start. Her candid comments and offbeat humor helped make this book possible. Don George made suggestions for a new species, the Gearhead Geezer. And Tom Lee, an all-purpose Renaissance geezer if there ever was one, provided much material for this guide. I was blessed to share his wit and humor and technical support through many seasons of my research.

Because my research took nearly thirty years, a few of the above-mentioned friends are no longer with us.

Alana Sholar contributed cowboy geezerisms. Carol Oberton told me about geezers she met while traveling, with names like Dugout Dick. Steve Reugge brought wit and stories from "The Street of Dreams." And I've been blessed to be in a writing group with four women who offered quips and constructive criticism that helped shape the final product. Heartfelt thanks to Sue Erickson, Nancy Canyon, C. J. Prince, and Carol Austin. Both Pam Beason and my beautiful

daughter-in-law, Lee Suttorp, kindly provided
major computer aid.

Special thanks to Bobbie Ryder Johanson and
Karl Johanson for time at their "Vinyl Villa" near
Sandpoint, Idaho, where I finally finished this
guidebook.

About the Author

As the daughter of a stump rancher and "powder monkey" named Post Hole Augerson, Rae Ellen's enthusiasm for geezers began at an early age. She carefully charted the activities of geezers

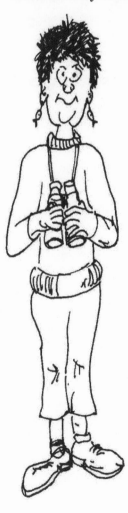

everywhere life took her. She further honed viewing techniques while working as a landscape architect with the U.S. Forest Service, an agency of unusual species richness. Now a grandmother, Rae Ellen spends summer months stalking her prey in Northern Idaho and Montana, and the rest of the year exploring the canyons of the southwestern U.S. with her canine companion, Suds Terkel. Look for her at cowboy poetry events, antique tractor shows, harmonica festivals and wherever else geezers can be found.

Find more information on her books and whereabouts at **www.raeellenlee.com**.

About the Illustrator

John A. Alley is a native and resident of Butte, Montana, a rugged mining town on the flanks of the Continental Divide.

As an apprentice geezer, John worked as an attendant in a root beer stand; a drill oiler in an open pit mine; a student at several universities; an illustrator in the United States Army; a layout and darkroom tech for a printing shop; a graphic designer with an advertising studio; a visual information specialist for the U.S. Forest Service; and a custodian at a small state college.

John has a degree in graphic design from Montana State University. Now in his seventies, he has the age and weathering to qualify as a journeyman geezer in the creative division.

An Essential Companion to
A Field Guide to Geezers:

Powder Monkey Tales—A Portrait in Stories
By Wesley Moore alias Post Hole Augerson
As told to Rae Ellen Lee

This collection of authentic geezer stories captures the history and humor of Wesley Moore, alias Post Hole Augerson, a geezer of some renown. A farm boy from Illinois turned woods-worker in northern Idaho, Wes used dynamite to help build logging roads for Diamond (through three company name changes.) They called him a "powder monkey." We learn about Post Hole's childhood on a farm during The Depression, about his pet skunks and what happened the day he ate green grapes all the way to school. He tells about "jerking" five tons of sweet corn by noon, and later what life was like at Camp 9 near Priest Lake, Idaho. The stories are illustrated with select photos of days gone by. This booklet is available in print and for

Kindle via Amazon.com. Please visit the author's website for more info: **www.raeellenlee.com**. The following story from *Powder Monkey Tales* was performed at the Idaho Centennial Play in Pocatello, Idaho, in 1989—a significant honor for old Post Hole.

THE OSPREY AND THE FISHING LICENSE

One day I went down across the road here, perch fishing in the Pend Oreille River. I fished for a while and caught a few. Just down the river on the bank sat an osprey. One wing was hanging down. Looked like he was pretty weak. Must'a flew into the telephone line or something, hurt himself. So I took a couple fish down there, close as I could get. I tossed him one. He ate it. I tossed him another. He ate that one, too. I went back to where I was fishing, and he follered me. I gave him another fish when he got there. Oh, I fished a while longer and headed home. He follered me again. When I got home it was startin' to get a little dark. 'Bout time to go to roost anyway, so I took the osprey out to the shed and set him on the back of an old chair.

Went out in the morning, took him some more fish and a pan of water for a drink. He hung around here for a few days. I kept feeding him. Finally he got so he could fly around a little, and got used to flying again. Two or three days went by and he took off.

After that, every few days he'd bring me a mess of fish. Dropped 'em onto the porch one at a time. Kept that up for a couple weeks. One day the game warden caught him at it and said, "Wes, you're gonna have to buy that osprey a fishing license."

The Osprey and the Fishing License

OTHER BOOKS BY RAE ELLEN LEE

FICTION

THE BLUEBIRD HOUSE –
A Madam. A Diary. A Murder.

"*A western romance laced with dark comedy; this* Book is a wonder*ful read.*"
– Midwest Book Review

"*A mid-life makeover, courtesy of an angry moose. The first person narrative gives it the feeling of a memoir.*"
-- L. Burns, Vine™ Voice

After getting stepped on by a moose, middle-aged Molly is starting over. She buys an old Montana mining camp brothel to renovate and uncovers the story of the madam who once owned the place and ends up solving a cold case. A multi-genre feast one reviewer described as a paranormal historical romance adventure novel with a mystery and some mountain man recipes.

FICTION

CHEATING THE HOG –
A Sawmill. A Tragedy. A Few Gutsy Women.

"In the face of dangerous odds, Echo puts on her big-girl panties and her hard hat and proceeds to clean house."
– Sherry Gohr, avid reader

"A story that pulls you in, and keeps you there all the way to the end."
-- Penny Bews, Priest River

Echo is turning 50, and she's desperate. When the local sawmill hires her to do cleanup and odd jobs, like cheating the hog, she expects to be farting in silk–that is, after she pays off her gambling debt. But will this job kill her before she can collect her first paycheck?

MEMOIR

IF THE SHOE *FITS* (print); I ONLY *CUSS WHEN I'M SAILING* (E-book)

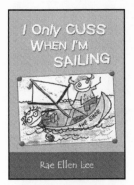

"A pure delight. Told with clarity, insight, straight-forward story-telling and remarkable humor." – Carol Hasse, sail maker

"... had me laughing (and) then crying within a few sentences." -- Glee, Amazon Reviewer

A Montana couple moves to the West Coast to fix up an old boat, learn to sail, and set forth to the Caribbean. But things don't go as planned. The book is about taking risks and making changes, told with a candid and humorous perspective.

MEMOIR

MY NEXT HUSBAND WILL BE NORMAL – *A St. John Adventure* (Sequel)

"What a read! I laughed out loud, was touched to tears, felt compassionate, and gained some great insight."
>--Christine M.,
>Santa Rosa, CA

"I laughed. I cried. What a ride. What a story!"
-- Kathryn Hamshar,
   Priest River, Idaho

The couple abandons the sailboat and flies to St. John, USVI, where they buy a business. But soon after unpacking their flip-flops the husband realizes *he* is really a *she*. Told with a generous heart. a tragicomic style, and a cast of colorful cats, customers, and Caribbean personalities. Toss in a few sex toys, some steel pan music, a pinch of voodoo. . . and stir.

Blank page for notes.

21613784R00069

Made in the USA
Charleston, SC
26 August 2013